POLLUTION

IN INFOGRAPHICS

Envir◉Graphics

Published in the United States of America by Cherry Lake Publishing Group
Ann Arbor, Michigan
www.cherrylakepublishing.com

Reading Adviser: Marla Conn, MS, Ed., Literacy specialist, Read-Ability, Inc.
Photo Credits: ©Shutterstock, cover; ©Shutterstock, 1; ©Shutterstock, 4; ©Shutterstock, 5; ©Shutterstock, 8; ©Shutterstock, 9; ©Shutterstock, 10; ©Shutterstock, 12; ©Shutterstock, 13; ©Clker-Free-Vector-Images/ Pixabay, 13; ©Shutterstock, 14; ©Shutterstock, 15; ©Shutterstock, 16; ©Shutterstock, 17; ©Shutterstock, 19; ©Shutterstock, 20; ©Henry Frank Moore/Wikimedia, 21; ©Shutterstock, 21; ©Shutterstock, 22; ©Shutterstock, 23; ©Alefonte/Pixabay, 23; ©Yuri_B/Pixabay, 23; ©Shutterstock, 24; ©Shutterstock, 26; ©Shutterstock, 27; ©Shutterstock, 28; ©Shutterstock, 29; ©itman__47/iStock/Getty Images, 30

Cherry Lake Press is an imprint of Cherry Lake Publishing Group.

Library of Congress Cataloging-in-Publication Data has been filed and is available at catalog.loc.gov

Cherry Lake Publishing Group would like to acknowledge the work of the
Partnership for 21st Century Learning, a Network of Battelle for Kids. Please
visit http://www.battelleforkids.org/networks/p21 for more information.

Printed in the United States of America
Corporate Graphics

TABLE OF CONTENTS

INTRODUCTION

What Is Pollution? 4

CHAPTER 1

Types of Pollution 6

CHAPTER 2

Dangers of Pollution 12

CHAPTER 3

Protecting the Planet........................ 16

CHAPTER 4

Where and How to Help....................24

ACTIVITY.. 30

LEARN MORE 31

GLOSSARY 32

INDEX.. 32

What Is Pollution?

Pollution happens when harmful substances are put into the world. These substances can be waste or chemicals. Pollution is anything that makes Earth unhealthy.

[21ST CENTURY SKILLS LIBRARY]

 **AIR POLLUTION**

WATER POLLUTION

 **LAND POLLUTION**

CHAPTER 1

Types of Pollution

Air pollution happens when gases and smoke get into the air and make it unclean. It then becomes unsafe to breathe. Air pollution can cause many **respiratory** diseases. That means people get sick from breathing bad air. Air pollution can also fall back down to land. This can kill plants and animals.

HIGHEST PERCENTAGE OF DEATHS FROM AIR POLLUTION BY COUNTRY

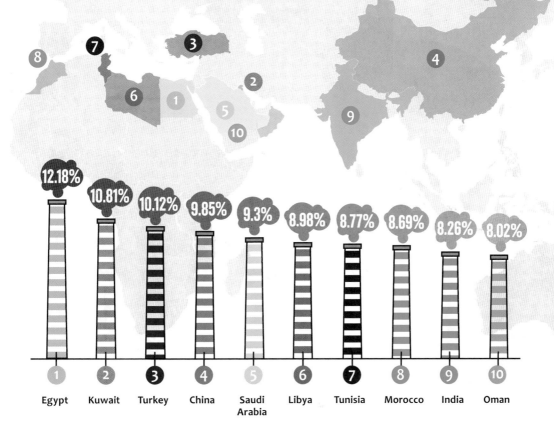

12.18%	10.81%	10.12%	9.85%	9.3%	8.98%	8.77%	8.69%	8.26%	8.02%
1	2	3	4	5	6	7	8	9	10
Egypt	Kuwait	Turkey	China	Saudi Arabia	Libya	Tunisia	Morocco	India	Oman

2019, Our World in Data

Water pollution happens when harmful objects get into water sources. Common objects are litter, such as plastic, and chemicals. This makes the water unsafe for people and animals to drink. Water pollution can come from runoff. Runoff is water from rain or snow that flows over the land instead of soaking into the soil. It can also come from **dumping**.

THE FOLLOWING FIGURES ARE TRUE FOR THE 21ST CENTURY

250 MILLION people contract diseases from **contaminated** water per year.

Unsafe water causes **4%** of all deaths worldwide.

Communicable diseases are the **#1 KILLER** of children under 5.

2013, Pacific Institute

THE BIGGEST OIL SPILLS IN HISTORY AS OF 2020

378
million gallons*

Lakeview Gusher
Kern County, California
1910–1911

160–420
million gallons

Gulf War Oil Spill
Persian Gulf
1991

138
million gallons

Ixtoc I
Gulf of Mexico
1979–1980

90
million gallons

**The Atlantic
Empress Disaster**
Atlantic Ocean
1979

134–206
million gallons

Deepwater Horizon
Gulf of Mexico
2010

1 gallon = 3.8 liters

2019, Britannica

TYPES OF LAND POLLUTION

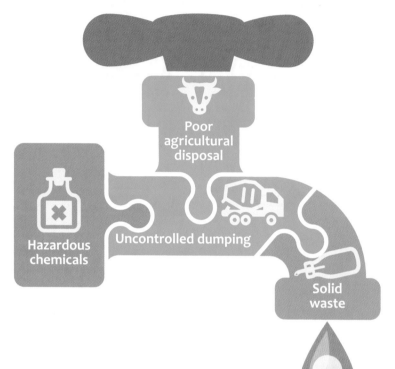

Poor agricultural disposal

Hazardous chemicals

Uncontrolled dumping

Solid waste

LAND POLLUTION IS A SEVERE THREAT

ENERGY PRODUCTION and **FOOD WASTE** make up about **80%** of land pollution.

400 MILLION TONS of **HAZARDOUS WASTE** is produced annually around the globe. This is one of the biggest acts of human pollution.

2018, Live Science

[21ST CENTURY SKILLS LIBRARY]

LEAST POLLUTED CITIES

The following cities are the least polluted on Earth. The scores include a point system for air quality, water pollution, and cleanliness. A score of "0" would mean no pollution.

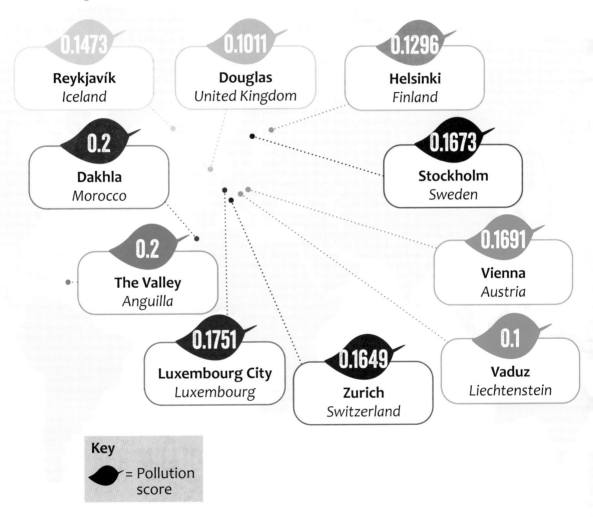

0.1473
Reykjavík
Iceland

0.1011
Douglas
United Kingdom

0.1296
Helsinki
Finland

0.2
Dakhla
Morocco

0.1673
Stockholm
Sweden

0.2
The Valley
Anguilla

0.1691
Vienna
Austria

0.1751
Luxembourg City
Luxembourg

0.1649
Zurich
Switzerland

0.1
Vaduz
Liechtenstein

Key
= Pollution score

2019, Global Residence Index

Dangers of Pollution

Throughout history, there have been **catastrophic** pollution events caused by humans. Pollution continues to have a large impact on the planet.

1500

1850

1900

Past 500 Years

About 1,000 species of animals have gone **extinct**.

1984

Union Carbide Methyl Isocyanate Leak: In India, a chemical leak killed around 5,000 people. It has since claimed as many as 20,000 more lives.

1952

London's Killer Fog: Over 12,000 people died in London, England, due to air pollution.

2050

Plant and animal loss continues to accelerate.

2000

1950

2050

1986

Chernobyl: A **nuclear plant** explosion led to more than 9,000 cancer deaths.

Present

Extinction rates are 10 times higher than they have been in the past 10 million years.

2019, New York Times

TOTAL ANNUAL POLLUTION-RELATED DEATHS

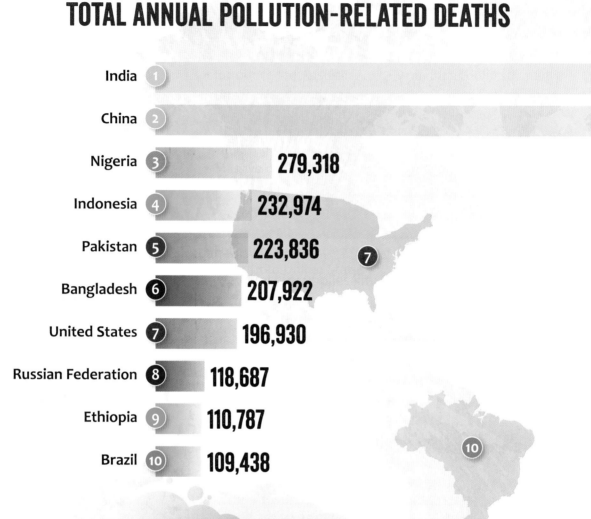

India (1)

China (2)

Nigeria (3) **279,318**

Indonesia (4) **232,974**

Pakistan (5) **223,836**

Bangladesh (6) **207,922**

United States (7) **196,930**

Russian Federation (8) **118,687**

Ethiopia (9) **110,787**

Brazil (10) **109,438**

2019, Global Alliance on Health and Pollution

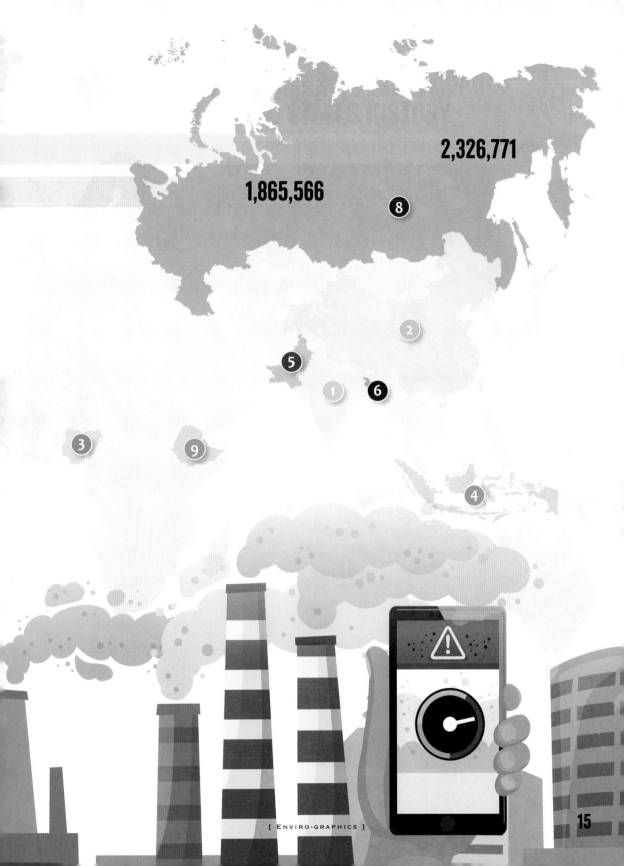

2,326,771

1,865,566

Protecting the Planet

In the United States between ■ 1980 and ■ 2018, the amount of every air pollutant has lessened.

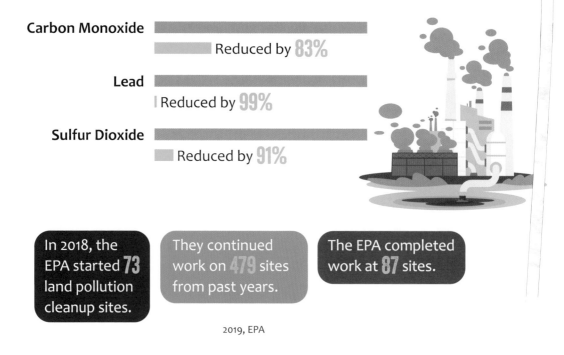

Carbon Monoxide
Reduced by **83%**

Lead
Reduced by **99%**

Sulfur Dioxide
Reduced by **91%**

In 2018, the EPA started **73** land pollution cleanup sites.

They continued work on **479** sites from past years.

The EPA completed work at **87** sites.

2019, EPA

TIMELINE

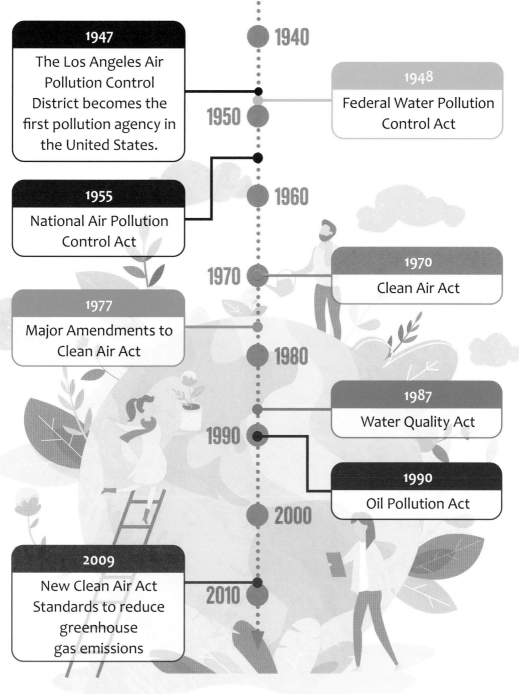

1940

1947
The Los Angeles Air Pollution Control District becomes the first pollution agency in the United States.

1950

1948
Federal Water Pollution Control Act

1955
National Air Pollution Control Act

1960

1970

1970
Clean Air Act

1977
Major Amendments to Clean Air Act

1980

1987
Water Quality Act

1990

1990
Oil Pollution Act

2000

2009
New Clean Air Act Standards to reduce greenhouse gas emissions

2010

COMBATING AIR POLLUTION

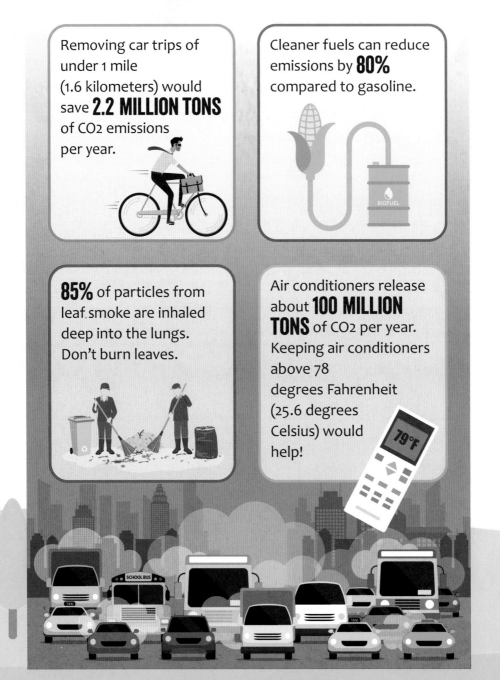

Removing car trips of under 1 mile (1.6 kilometers) would save **2.2 MILLION TONS** of CO2 emissions per year.

Cleaner fuels can reduce emissions by **80%** compared to gasoline.

BIOFUEL

85% of particles from leaf smoke are inhaled deep into the lungs. Don't burn leaves.

Air conditioners release about **100 MILLION TONS** of CO2 per year. Keeping air conditioners above 78 degrees Fahrenheit (25.6 degrees Celsius) would help!

79°F

SCHOOL BUS

TAXI

TAXI

2019, New York Times

HOW ELECTRIC CARS WORK

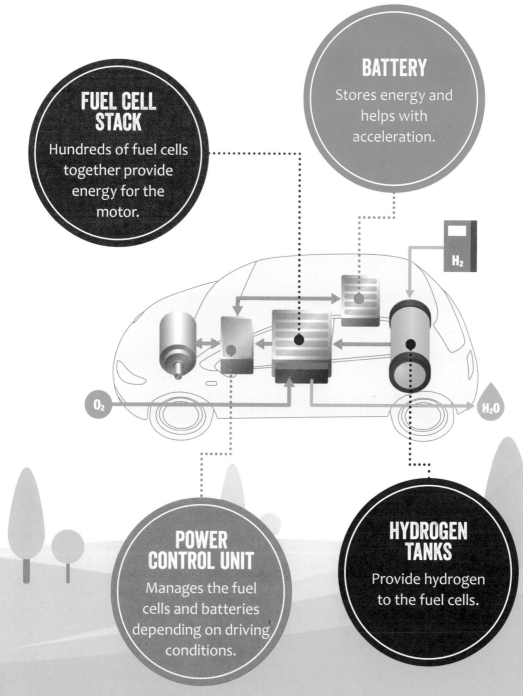

FUEL CELL STACK
Hundreds of fuel cells together provide energy for the motor.

BATTERY
Stores energy and helps with acceleration.

POWER CONTROL UNIT
Manages the fuel cells and batteries depending on driving conditions.

HYDROGEN TANKS
Provide hydrogen to the fuel cells.

O_2

H_2

H_2O

Plastic pollution affects 267 different types of animals. Plastic makes up as much as 95 percent of land debris in water pollution.

HOW TO KEEP WATER CLEAN

Don't flush things down the toilet or sink.

Avoid using a garbage disposal.

Run the dishwasher and washing machines less often.

Don't use pesticides.

Don't pour oil down the sink.

2020, Clean Water Action

OYSTERS

Oysters are one type of animal that helps filter water. More oysters in a water source can lead to cleaner water.

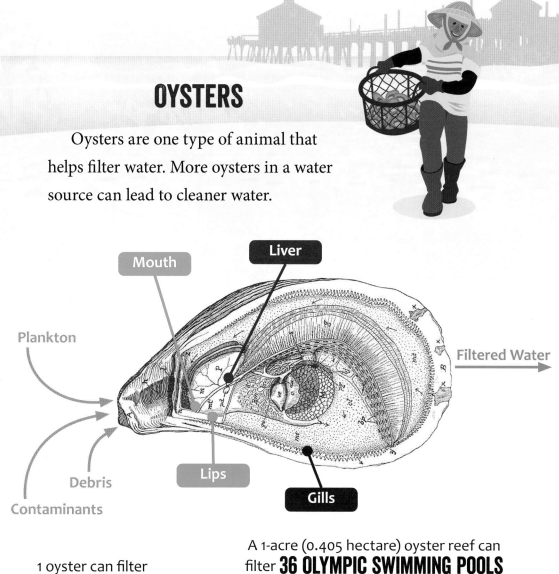

Mouth

Liver

Plankton

Filtered Water

Debris

Lips

Contaminants

Gills

1 oyster can filter
50 GALLONS (189.271 L)
of water a day.

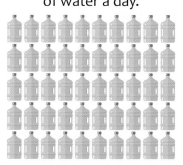

A 1-acre (0.405 hectare) oyster reef can filter **36 OLYMPIC SWIMMING POOLS** of water a day.

2008, Science Direct

The average American generates 4.5 pounds (2 kilograms) of household trash per day. About 52 percent of that ends up at the dump.

EACH PERSON SENDS NEARLY 850 POUNDS* OF TRASH TO THE DUMP ANNUALLY.

*1 pound = 0.45 kilograms

2016, Rubbish Please

Plastic is one of the biggest pollutants. There are many materials that are more environmentally friendly that can replace plastic.

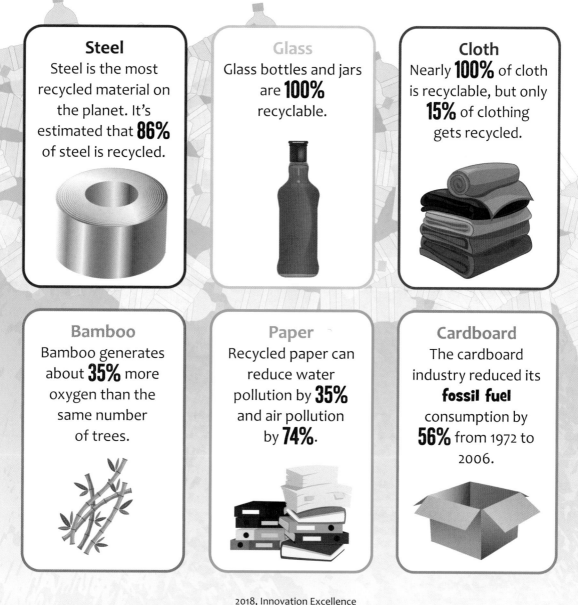

Steel
Steel is the most recycled material on the planet. It's estimated that **86%** of steel is recycled.

Glass
Glass bottles and jars are **100%** recyclable.

Cloth
Nearly **100%** of cloth is recyclable, but only **15%** of clothing gets recycled.

Bamboo
Bamboo generates about **35%** more oxygen than the same number of trees.

Paper
Recycled paper can reduce water pollution by **35%** and air pollution by **74%**.

Cardboard
The cardboard industry reduced its **fossil fuel** consumption by **56%** from 1972 to 2006.

2018, Innovation Excellence

CHAPTER 4

Where and
How to Help

Some cities in the United States have far worse pollution than other places. Often, this pollution is caused by **stagnant air** and by factories running for many years.

WORST AIR POLLUTION

Pollution is measured in Air Quality Index. The higher the number, the dirtier the air. High levels of polluted air can make people sick. The closer the number is to 0, the better the air quality is.

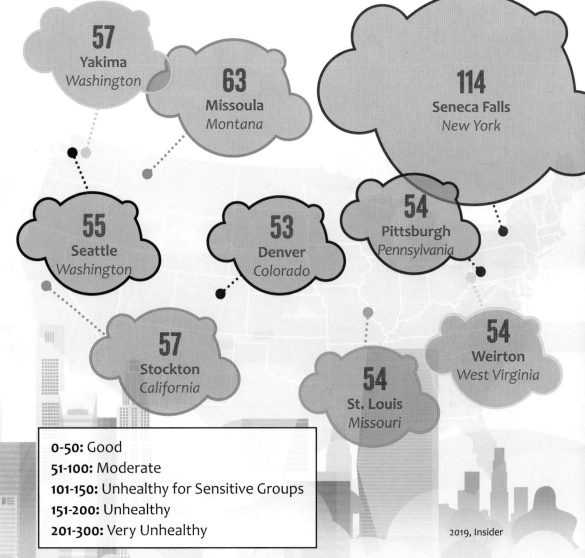

57
Yakima
Washington

63
Missoula
Montana

114
Seneca Falls
New York

55
Seattle
Washington

53
Denver
Colorado

54
Pittsburgh
Pennsylvania

54
Weirton
West Virginia

57
Stockton
California

54
St. Louis
Missouri

0-50: Good
51-100: Moderate
101-150: Unhealthy for Sensitive Groups
151-200: Unhealthy
201-300: Very Unhealthy

2019, Insider

WAYS TO STOP POLLUTION

1

Friends of the Earth

This organization provides kits in the United Kingdom to let citizens test air quality.

2

Vertical Forest

In China, there are plans for the Nanjing Vertical Forest to help purify the air.

3

Free Transportation

Germany is considering making public transportation free for everyone.

4

CityTree

This billboard-like object can filter the same amount of carbon dioxide as 275 trees.

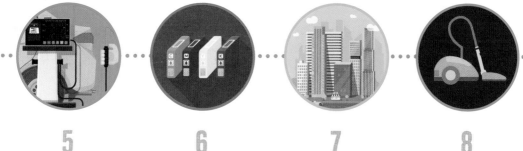

| 5 | 6 | 7 | 8 |

Pollution Sensors

In India, sensors are being put all over the country to help make citizens aware of air pollution.

AIR-INK

Printer ink can be made from carbon emissions.

Xian Air Purifier

In China, a 328-foot (100 meters) tall building is going to be used as an air purifier.

Pollution Vacuum Cleaners

Dutch inventors have found a way for giant industrial vacuums to suck up air pollution.

2019, Interesting Engineering

WHAT CAN WE DO?

TAKE PUBLIC TRANSPORTATION TO WORK

Commuting with public transportation saves 4,800 pounds (2,177 kg) of CO2 per person per year.

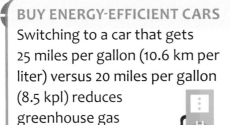

BUY ENERGY-EFFICIENT CARS

Switching to a car that gets 25 miles per gallon (10.6 km per liter) versus 20 miles per gallon (8.5 kpl) reduces greenhouse gas emissions by 1.7 tons annually.

EAT LESS MEAT
Raising cows, pigs, and chickens produces as much greenhouse gas as all the cars on Earth combined.

AVOID PURCHASING PRODUCTS IN PLASTIC
The average American uses 220 pounds (100 kg) of plastic per year.

USE SOLAR PANELS
One solar panel can cover an average of 5% of a home's energy needs.

WATER FILTRATION EXPERIMENT

Materials:

- Dirty water
- A plastic cup with a hole cut in the bottom
- 3 to 4 coffee filters
- Sand
- Gravel
- 2 glass jars

1. Get a cup of dirty water. Usually, pond or puddle water can be used.

2. In the plastic cup with a hole in the bottom, put coffee filters. Add clean sand on top of them, then a layer of gravel.

3. Put that cup on top of an empty jar.

4. Pour the dirty water through the cup with the sand, gravel, and filters.

5. Look at how the new water is much cleaner.

Learn More

BOOKS

French, Jess. *What a Waste: Trash, Recycling, and Protecting our Planet.* New York, NY: DK Publishing, 2019

Reilly, Kathleen M. *Planet Earth: Finding Balance on the Blue Marble.* White River Junction, VT: Nomad Press, 2019.

Wilson, Janet. *Our Future: How Kids Are Taking Action.* Toronto, ON: Second Story Press, 2019.

WEBSITES

Britannica Kids
https://kids.britannica.com/kids/article/pollution/353650

Ducksters
https://www.ducksters.com/science/environment/air_pollution.php

National Geographic Kids
https://kids.nationalgeographic.com/explore/science/pollution

BIBLIOGRAPHY

Environmental Protection Agency. "Air Quality-National Summary." Last modified January 1, 2019. https://www.epa.gov/air-trends/air-quality-national-summary

Global Alliance on Health and Pollution. "New Report Pollution and Health Metrics: Global, Regional, and Country Analysis." Last modified December 31, 2019. https://gahp.net/pollution-and-health-metrics

Rubbish Please. "Land Pollution Facts and Statistics." Last modified June 1, 2016. https://rubbishplease.co.uk/blog/land-pollution-facts-statistics

GLOSSARY

catastrophic (kat-uh-STRAH-fik) an event that caused great damage or suffering

communicable diseases (kuh-MYOO-nih-kuh-bul dih-ZEE-zez) infectious diseases that are spread through direct contact

contaminated (kuhn-TAM-ih-nay-tid) made dirty or impure because something harmful was added

dumping (DUHM-ping) throwing garbage or waste onto the ground in large amounts

extinct (eks-TINGKT) when there are no living members of a specific species

fossil fuel (FAH-suhl FYOOL) a natural fuel such as gas or coal that is sourced from Earth

nuclear plant (NOO-klee-ur PLANT) a facility that uses a nuclear reactor as a source of heat to generate thermal power and produce electricity

respiratory (RES-pruh-toh-ree) relating to the breathing system of the body

stagnant air (STAG-nent AIR) air that has no movement or flow

INDEX

air, 5, 6, 7–8, 11, 13, 16, 17, 18, 23, 24, 25, 26, 27
Air Quality Index, 25

chemicals, 4, 8, 10

diseases, 6, 8

emissions, 17, 18, 27, 28
Environmental Protection Agency (EPA), 16

greenhouse gas, 17, 28, 29

land, 5, 6, 8, 10, 16, 20
litter. *See* waste

oil spills, 9

plastic, 8, 20, 23, 29

recycling, 23

trash. *See* waste

waste, 4, 8, 10, 22
water, 5, 8, 11, 17, 20, 21, 23

ABOUT THE AUTHOR

Alexander Lowe is a writer who splits his time between Los Angeles and Chicago. He has written children's books about sports, technology, science, and media. He has also done extensive work as a sportswriter and film critic. He loves reading books of any and all kinds.